A Group of Critters

written by
Steve McAllister

artwork by
Anita Wexler
Van Jazmin
& Vicki Squires

www.stevemc.xyz
@Steve McAlphabet
ISBN - 978-1-7346910-8-5
Copyright 2023

Back in the late Middle Ages, they came up with this concept of venery.

It started somewhere in France in about the 14th century.

It seems that the wealthy hunters wanted new ways to name their game,

possibly in the wild hope that it might improve their aim.

The tradition caught on with others and the game it started to spread,

**so instead of just saying, "There's a group of critters,"
they called them this instead...**

A group of buffalo is an obstinacy

and kangaroos are mobs

elk form gangs

snakes make nests

and dolphins swim in pods

monkeys come in barrels

and pigs, they love their passels

goldfish are a troubling

but they're really not a hassle

woodpeckers are in a descent

woodpeckers are in a descent

and there's a nice bouquet of pheasant

starlings dance in murmurations

when more than one are present

bullfinches like to bellow

and peacocks have their ostentations

geese, they tend to gaggle

and eagles meet in convocations

there's a conspiracy of those lemurs

around the murder of the crows

around the murder of the crows

and while guinea fowl are a confusion

try to untie a knot of toads

jaguars move in shadows

and lions have their prides

buzzards hold a wake

porcupines prickle

and bees, they live in hives

bats are found in cauldrons

bats are found in cauldrons

and cobras coil in a quiver

and sharks, they make you shiver

foxes skulk

donkeys follow pace

and crabs have their consortiums

owls hold a parliament

and cockroaches are an intrusion

litters are for kittens

but cats, they come in clowders

clams are found lying in beds

but are much better in chowders

most fish go to school

but trout just like to hover

but trout just like to hover

while nightingales tend to watch

coots, they have a cover

ferrets are a business

apes they come in shrewdness

upon a sloth of bears

tigers are an ambush

and they're lurking everywhere

parrots are a pandemonium

and there's a thunder of hippopotamuses

hyenas like to cackle

at the crash of rhinoceroses

armies are for caterpillars, herring...

frogs and ants

there are many tribes of goats

but parades are for elephants

platypi are in a puddle

gators form in congregations

cheetahs have coalitions

wombats wisdoms

larks sing in exaltations

it's quite a labor for moles

giraffes, they form a tower

while grasshoppers come in a cloud

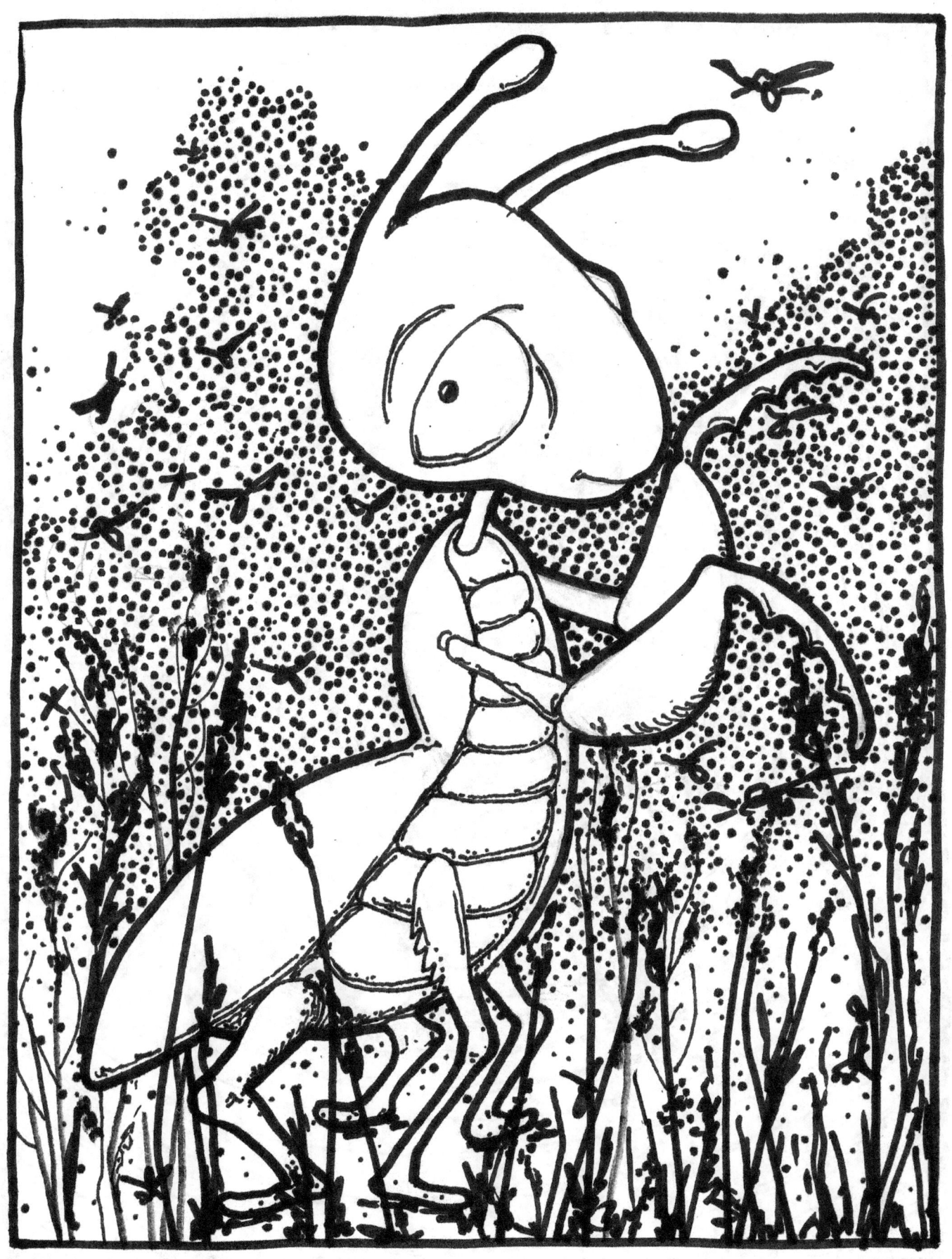

ducks fly in a flock

but they're a raft if they're on water

while leopards like to leap

to get a romp, you need some otters

squirrels know how to scurry

and rabbits form their warrens

have a gulp of cormorants

or try a siege of herons

it's a pitying for turtle doves

and gorillas form a band

there's a kaleidoscope of butterflies

there's a kaleidoscope of butterflies

and flamingos like to stand

there's a flock of sheep

a jellyfish bloom

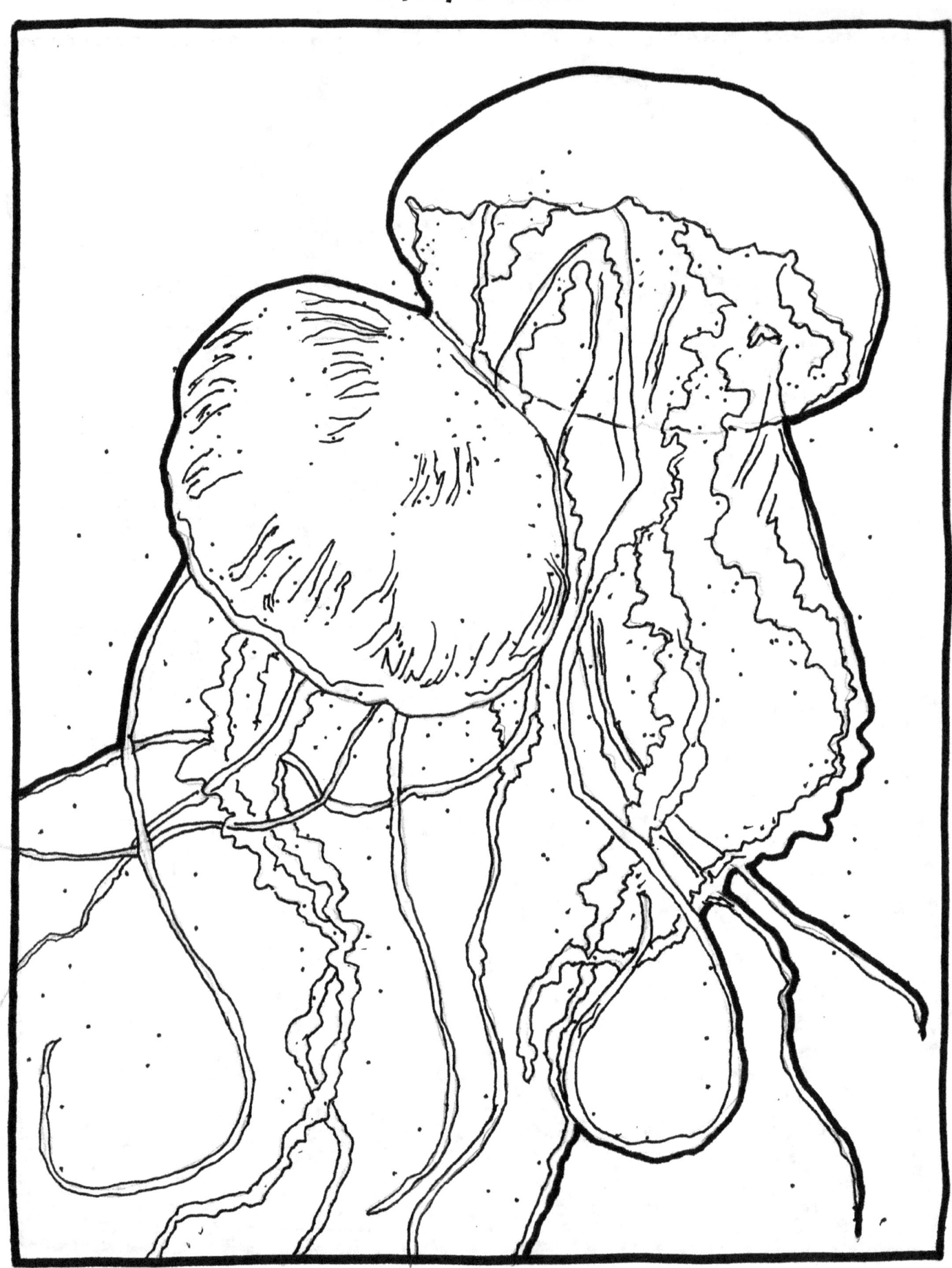

and martens have their richness

and while ravens are known for unkindness

who wouldn't love a charm of finches?

penguins live in colonies

and quails are in their coveys

jays throw parties

weasels sneak

and swans, they have their bevies

snails have hoods

lobsters are a risk

and zebras do have zeal

just remember that all of these critters

are more than just for meals

that's what I know about venery, and I hope you like what I did

because I'll never get a round of applause from an audience of squid

As an ABC Squared Economics project,
promoting Artistry, Business, Citizenry, and Community
a portion of all proceeds from *A Group of Critters*
will be donated to organizations
dedicated to animal welfare and wildlife conservation.
Watch the videos and get more information about
"A Group of Critters" at www.steve mc.xyz

ABOUT THE ARTISTS

Steve McAllister (also known as Steve McAlphabet) is a multi-faceted artist from Sarasota, Florida. He has been known as an actor, author, comedian, filmmaker, poet, singer, songwriter, and a really entertaining tour guide.
www.stevemc.xyz

Anita Wexler is a fine artist, teacher, sculptor, muralist, illustrator, and mixed media visual artist from Sarasota, Florida.
www.anitawexler.com

Van Jazmin is a multimedia artist and clown based in Los Angeles. He is a graduate of the Ringling College of Art and Design in Sarasota, FL (Circus Town USA).
www.vanjazmin.com

Vicki Squires describes herself as a "blue haired old lady who draws pictures" in Anna Maria, Florida.

www.ingramcontent.com/pod-product-compliance
Lightning Source LLC
Chambersburg PA
CBHW081405070526
44583CB00020B/2684